Seven Essential Practices for the Professional Artist

Michele Théberge

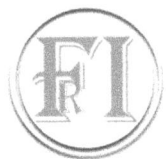

© Michele Théberge, 2013
Images, artworks and text by Michele Théberge
Except backcover photo by Sibila Savage

www.micheletheberge.com

Published by F. Issaly (Editions FrI)

Théberge, Michele - 1964
Texts in English

ISBN-10: 0981186068
ISBN-13: 978-0-9811860-6-1

"There are so many people who need this tool and would benefit from what you're offering! Many of the people I work with as coaching clients don't have "mechanical" issues or obstacles to their studio practice or marketing--but they really do have spiritual and emotional blocks, and I think your approach would really help them."

- Jamie Brunson, artist, teacher, independent curator

"Thanks to reading your book I feel more encouraged and focus and going out and showing my work. Sometimes I believe part of being afraid in moving forward from my work was the fact of the belief in "starving artist" now I truly believe I can if I put my all into it."

- Rocio Mora, artist

"I couldn't stop reading it and it really changed my perspective. I had been struggling with a block the last couple of months, overwhelmed with work but not getting much done. It was life changing to read about another artist's struggles with the same thing, and learn how you overcame them.

I tried the 20 minute routine today and it worked so well! It made me conscious of when I was starting to lose focus (and as a result, waste time) on a task, which is incredibly valuable. Thank you for sharing your knowledge with us, it is invaluable and I just wanted to let you know that I really, really appreciate it!"

- Lauren Elizabeth, artist

"I want to thank you for the book, a lot of deep emotion and valuable information to help carry me to that next level of establishing my work and work ethic as an artist."

- Matthew J. Johnson

"I love the piece about the wall. I hit that wall a couple of weeks ago, when I destroyed a large piece I was working on and had put days and hours into it. I just couldn't see the big picture, so I ripped it up! I don't know what made me feel worse! Not being able to get to the next step in it or throwing it away! I wish I had the benefit of knowing about the wall, it would have saved me some great stress!"

- Indigene Gaskin, artist

CONTENTS

ACKNOWLEDGMENTS

I am grateful for the generosity and thoughtfulness of all the people who took the time to offer their feedback, edits, proofreading, perspective and encouragement, including: Christy Chan, Alison deGroot, Anna Garrett, Ursula Jorch, Christine Kane, Colleen O'Grady, Lisa Michel, Sue Sullivan and Deanna Scoggin Torra.

I am so thankful that Françoise Issaly – an inspirational woman, artist and publisher – for believing in this book and helping carry these ideas out into the world.

And lastly, my depth of gratitude for my husband Jay is immeasurable. His love, caring, friendship, laughter and support have so reassuringly enfolded me all these years and offered a stable foundation for my all my creative endeavors.

INTRODUCTION

Perhaps you have been making art for a long time or maybe it is a new passion for you. A lot has been written about the making of art and the business side of being an artist, but just how does one carry on the *life* of a person who makes art? How does one maintain and nurture a creative practice for the long term, allowing it to grow and evolve over time? How does one balance the studio time with the time attending to marketing and business?

I had my own challenges with these questions. In my early years as an artist, I was determined and enthusiastic, yet suffered from debilitating self-doubts that impaired me both in the studio and in the business side of my art.

Immediately after I graduated from college in Boston, I moved out to California. I was thousands of miles away from my teachers and colleagues, so I had no one to guide and mentor me as I began my life as an artist. I bumbled along, taking every class and reading every book I could find about being a professional artist. These courses and books offered similar advice, but did not offer any clue as to how to develop either the confidence, nor a clear strategy of how to follow through on that advice.

I did submit my portfolio and enter shows here and there, but I had a random, inconsistent approach. There were galleries genuinely interested in my work, but I never followed up with them!

During this same period, I was on a path of personal growth. I began a daily meditation practice that continues to thrive and support me over twenty years later. I delved into yoga, psychotherapy and spiritual and philosophical teachings. These studies led to a solid foundation that has deeply influenced how I approach everything I do, including my studio practice and my career as an artist.

I learned to become more conscious and examine my thinking patterns. I was able to observe how *my thoughts alone,* and not solely my actions, were affecting my experiences. I had to come to terms with the humbling fact that I, alone, was responsible for holding back my success.

I couldn't hang my lack of professional success on what I had previously *perceived* as the problem – biased curators, unapproachable galleries, an art world full of elitism and favoritism. I had to let all that thinking go and focus purely on my own thoughts and subconscious beliefs.

Over time, I began to understand how my self-doubts were inhibiting action, how my negative attitudes and resentful perceptions of the art world were affecting my reception there. I also began to realize how much I was buying into the "starving artist" myth reinforced in the popular media, and how deeply detrimental this psychology is to all artists.

I started to think differently about my work and its place in the world.

As a young artist, I struggled to reconcile myself to the art world I had been exposed to in school, which primarily presented art as a luxury commodity. To be successful was to have work sold in an elite circle of galleries, museums and collectors. I felt outside of that world and did not relate to it. I was at odds with myself because although I wanted to sell my work, I was afraid that by participating in that exchange I was somehow perpetuating an economic disparity that deeply troubled me.

At the time, I failed to see how art has a much greater cultural impact that extends far beyond its life as a commodity. I was entrenched in a polarized thinking seeing the world as a dichotomy of rich and poor, powerful and powerless. (I, of course, perceived myself in the powerless and poor camp.)

Over time, I began to seriously examine my polarized thinking. I began to think less in black and white terms: good guys, bad guys, rich, and poor.

Much writing on art has to do with its external impact in the world. We live in a very materially focused world where so many people are focused purely on the tangible, measurable outcomes of their work. Is it selling? Is it creating change we can measure? Is it educating? Does it tell a story? What is its monetary value in the market? When we only look at the external impact of work we lose some of art's deepest gifts. Every day in studios, museums, galleries and public places the viewing of art and the making of art is having a profound impact on millions of lives. But it is that subtle internal impact that often goes unnoted and is nearly impossible to quantify.

As I became less externally focused and began to cultivate more inner awareness, I began to understand both the internal value and the transformational power of artwork. This allowed me to see art in a new way. I came to understand that what I place value on in my life and work – uplifting, inspiring or enlightening others with what I do - may have no measurable or tangible results.

I began to embrace the value of my work and ceased to worry about those who weren't interested in it. This new attitude inspired new action on behalf of my art. I began to have more faith and confidence in my work that was not contingent upon the approbation of others.

As a result of my gain in confidence and my ability to value my work independently of the opinions of others, the reception of my art began to change. Sales came more easily.

Galleries started seeking me out rather than me pursuing them. In addition, I *created* opportunities for myself, through many of the habits and practices outlined in this book that I now teach other artists. This led to my art being shown in exhibitions around the globe, my first museum shows, and countless other opportunities.

As a teacher, I naturally wanted to share these ideas with others, so I developed a mentorship program for artists and decided to write this book to help other artists achieve this same shift.

The intent of this book is to share the habits, practices and ways of thinking that have allowed me to maintain a creative practice for over two decades through the inevitable ups and downs, the successes, and the not quite successes.

This book is for you if:

You wish to call yourself artist but haven't found the courage *yet* to embrace that identity.

You absolutely love making art but can never seem to find time for it —those for whom everything else in life seems to come first, who struggle with prioritizing in their busy lives.

You are coming back to art after being away from it for a long time. You are determined not to let your passion take a backseat again.

You have established yourself as an artist, yet falter when it comes to following through on opportunities to get your work shown and to generate income from your passion.

You who wish your studio practice were more regular and predictable this book is to lead you to a path of more ease and flow with your creative practice.

If you are a self-doubter please know you are not alone! I'd like to sit and hold your hand and have a little words-on-paper "chat" with you, for I know this internal voice all too well. It may never leave you entirely but my wish is that you never again let it stop you in your tracks.

With this book, my desire is to support you in either your commitment or your recommitment to your creative practice.

Michele Théberge
Oakland, California
2013

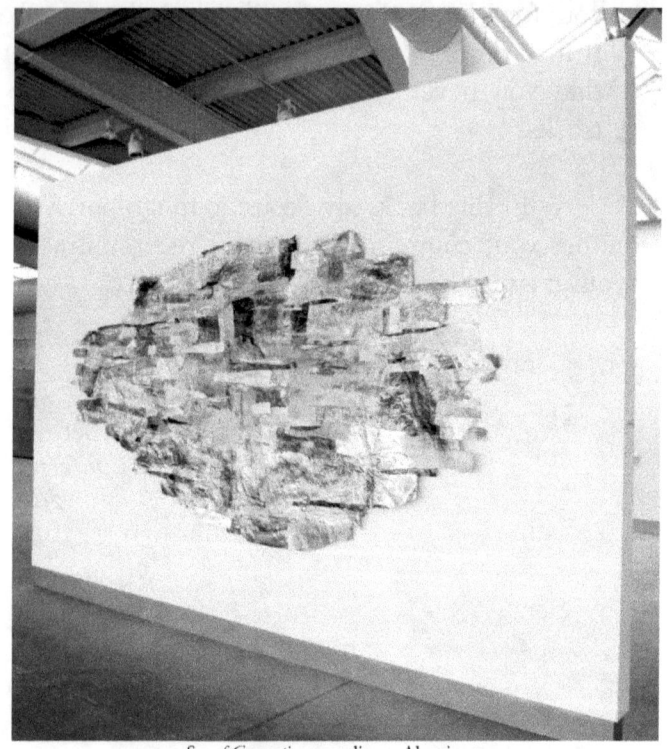

Sea of Connections, acrylic on Aluminum

1. Create a Studio Habit

Getting in the studio should be easy – it's what you love to do, right? Unfortunately, many artists have a uneasy on-again, off-again relationship with their studio practice.

We artists have important work to do in the world and valuable ideas to share. Anytime that work is not brought forth due to lack of confidence, organization, commitment or follow-through, it is a loss to society. It is not just the Chagalls and the Warhols that have something valuable to contribute. Every artist has a raw genius worth honing and refining through consistent work habits.

For some artists, it's difficult just to get into the studio and they are plagued with energy-draining guilt over it. Others get in the studio, but once there, have difficulty getting started. Many more are plagued by dark, crushing critical voices. Why do you suppose many famous artists in the '50s were notorious for heavy drinking?

When I start working with the artists I mentor, the crux of my program is to get everyone immediately started with a regular studio practice. But first, we have to clear the thought patterns and habits that have been standing in the way.

Through the years, I have developed tools to deal with the inner critic, practices to jump-start creativity, and methods for reflection and observation that have truly changed my studio practice. I encourage artists to cultivate a reverence and respect for inviolable studio time. Even if your practice is more conceptual or project-based, you can still schedule regular time to write, research, brainstorm or work on ideas to keep the creative mind in shape, alert and *well oiled*. Even the smallest increments of time can make a huge difference.

Creativity is like a muscle – use it regularly and it gets stronger, firmer, more toned and ready for action. But if you only work out in fits and spurts, – you won't be present and prepared when inspiration strikes. You won't be able to advance to the next level, and you'll miss the satisfaction of noticeable shifts and tangible results.

What the artists in the Mindful Artist Mentorship Program have learned is that studio practice is like a loyal friend. The connection to your practice is what pulls you through the tough times. If you love what you do and you are really connected to your creativity through a consistent practice, – you are less thrown off by rejection, or lack of support. Artists who work with me have reported feeling more confidence and clarity in the work as a result of establishing a regular studio practice. A Berkeley, California artist who went through the program, shared that she had discovered a connective thread in the work that she had not previously known was there. Through consistent practice, you will know the value of the creative process to your very core and understand that your work will consistently evolve and change over time. You will be able to ride the dry spells and difficult times with more equanimity. You will also be able to revel in those peak moments when your creative genius shines through.

A lot of artists focus on whether their work is selling and receiving attention or recognition as a measure of their success. That kind of outward focus is a creativity squelcher. If you are looking toward something outside of yourself to validate your work, such as sales, exhibitions or accolades, it will be hard to maintain your creative practice during the inevitable up and down cycles of an artist's career. In order to maintain the motivation to develop a regular studio habit, it helps to develop a strong and sure understanding of the inherent value of your work whether it is currently experiencing popularity or not.

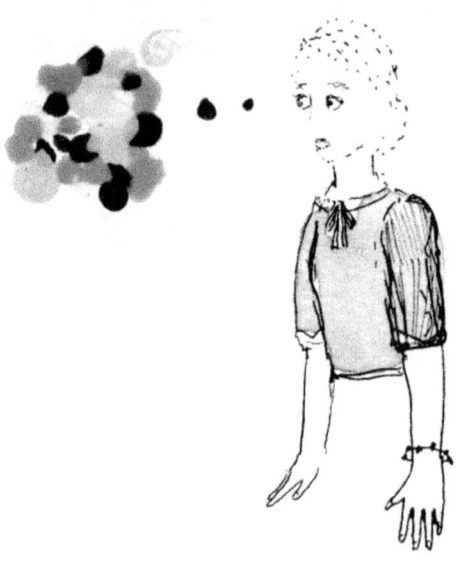

This Awful Mess, nail polish and ink on paper

2. Manage Your Thoughts

Our thoughts are everything. They can help us move us forward, energize and motivate us or they can sap enthusiasm, stifle creative output or ever stop us from working altogether.

Have you ever been working along happily on your art when all of a sudden you felt exhausted and drained for no apparent reason?

Have you experienced being unable to maintain your momentum because you are suddenly convinced that all your work is crap and you don't even know where to begin to fix it?

All of us have habits and patterns of thought that we unwittingly developed while young. These thoughts literally become like grooves in our brain – neural pathways – that create habits of self-criticism, fear, doubt, cynicism or worry that can be hard to break. When we learn how to manage our thoughts and catch them before an intense downward spiral begins, we can have a happier, more productive time in the studio.

When we are not conscious of the direction of our thoughts, we can get sucked down in a negative spiral. I teach artists who work with me specific processes for becoming more conscious of their thinking moment to moment, before the negativity gains momentum.

One of the processes I developed is the "Studio Check in". We set a timer to go off at twenty-minute intervals during a studio session and pause briefly to jot down our current feelings and thoughts. Without even *trying to change anything*, this practice brings a gentle, mindful awareness to our thought patterns so we have the option to choose more energizing and creative thoughts in the moment.

An artist from Washington state who went through the mentorship program, shares her experience: *"The Studio Check-in for me resulted in a newfound understanding that the state of mind that I go into when making art is not so fragile or delicate as I had imagined. Once engaged, I can set a timer and interrupt myself to see how it's going, and then return to wherever I was without really disturbing the flow. It was sort of like snorkeling, being completely engrossed in the beautiful underwater fish and coral, and then coming up to see where I was in relation to the shore. Of course, after surfacing I just want to dive in again, or if it's cold and there's a riptide, get out. During the check-in I would often write down new ideas and directions I would like to take the work I was engaged in. Without the checking in, these might have been forgotten."*

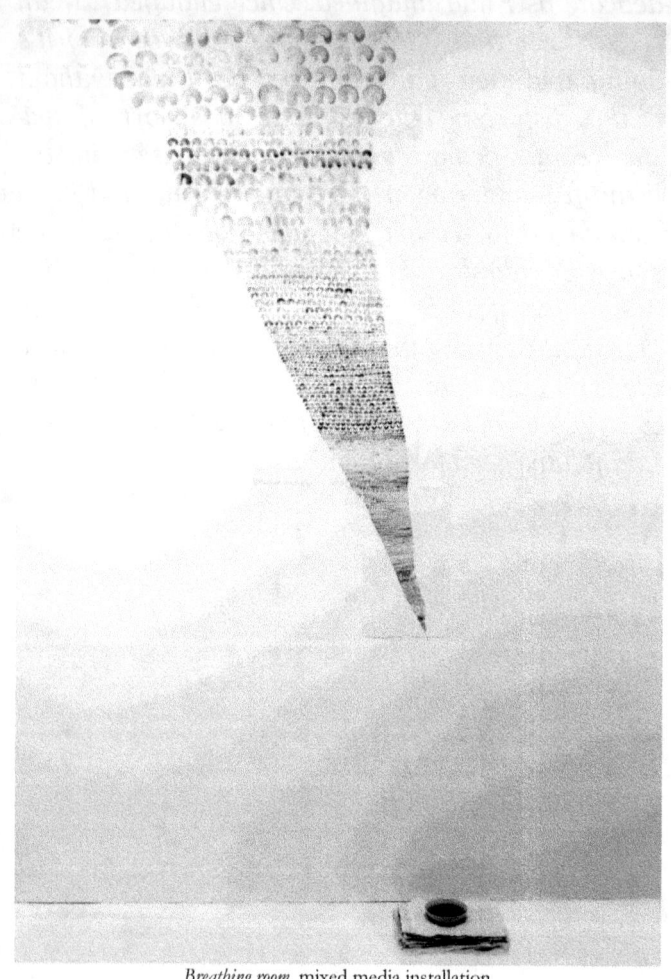

Breathing room, mixed media installation

3. Tap Into Yourself

I remember the shock when I first started taking advanced painting courses during my undergraduate studies. Before I went to art school, I had only studied in a typical American educational environment, diligently reading the required texts, taking notes, studying and following the teachers' assignments. Suddenly, I was in class and *no one was telling me what to do!* For the first time in my life, it was up to me what to paint and how to paint it.

I felt like the miller's daughter in the fairy tale, who was put in a room full of straw and told to spin it into gold. I had absolutely no idea how. And the funny thing was, hardly any of my teachers were much help with this. They couldn't teach me how to tap into myself, into my own ideas, and start a body of work or create a connection to my creative source.

It is not at all surprising to me that the majority of people have difficulties being creative. I've learned that encouraging innovative thinking can be taught, but most of us were raised in an environment that favored order, uniformity and memorizing existing information over originality, inventiveness and creative chaos.

Out of necessity, I became a keen student of creativity and the creative process. I began to observe and analyze how creative projects are born, developed and nurtured and also to learn what blocks or stifles the creative brain. I studied interviews with innovative artists and ingenious thinkers of all types, noting how they worked and what they said about their processes. I observed myself carefully in the studio, noting what worked and what didn't. When I taught, I paid close attention to the differences in creativity in children and adults (and they are vast!). I noted at what age the natural inborn creativity that I saw in young children dropped off. I researched different educational systems such as the schools in the Reggio Emilia region of Italy and was astounded at the creativity that can emerge when it is consciously cultivated.

What I learned has had a remarkable impact on my creativity. Now, instead of fits and starts in the studio, I have an unending stream of creative ideas and projects. So many, in fact, that I used to worry about having time and energy to bring into concrete form enormous flood of ideas that came into my head. Now, I write them all down and trust that the really important ones will be there when the time is right. I have noticed that an idea may come to fruition years later but it will take a different form than I had originally imagined because *I* have changed. I suggest that you, too, write down all of your ideas no matter how far-fetched, simplistic or ridiculous they may seem. No matter if you think you don't have time, money or resources for them right now. This is a way of acknowledging your creative mind for giving the ideas to you and encouraging it to generate more. Know that there will always be more ideas than you can execute, and simply savor that you have such a fertile, active mind.

Over the years, I have shared what I have learned about the creative process with artists who study with me. They, too, have learned what an extraordinary difference it makes just to have a deeper understanding of the normal phases of the creative process.

One of the biggest breakthroughs for me was to understand and embrace what I call "The Wall". No matter how many times I have faced it and passed through it, The Wall still catches me unaware. It's that moment, that hour, that week, that day, when you look at the project you have been laboring on and are convinced that it is utterly irretrievable or unsolvable, perhaps even worthless. You come to believe that all the work you have done was for naught and you had better just give up this whole business of being an artist because your work is no good, you will never amount to anything, you are wholly incompetent or totally lacking in talent or creativity. The initial blush of enthusiasm that started and fuelled the project is dead. *Where did the fun go?*

It's a horrible feeling.

And yet, it is a totally natural stage of the creative process.

Moreover, as unlikely as it may sound, there is a tremendous gift here. For when you get to this point, as uncomfortable as it may be, it means you are about to make a breakthrough in the work. This breakthrough will impact not only this one piece or project, but also all your work going into the future. This is where you truly grow and evolve as an artist.

However, you will be unable to move forward without some trust in the process. The first time you face these feelings, it will take tremendous faith to keep working in spite of them. As unreasonable as these self-doubts thoughts may appear as you are reading them now, when you are in the midst of The Wall, they feel like the absolute Truth.

This is where your commitment to practice comes in. This is when your community of support will help carry you through. You will need to step outside of your own thoughts and ego to move forward.

Allow the work to speak to you and tell you what it needs. Sometimes this will mean sitting quietly and reflecting on the work until a way becomes clear. Sometimes, there will be a dramatic shift in the work, other times a subtle change is needed. You may need to seek outside ideas and inspiration to know what to do. A visit to the museum or library, a talk with a friend, a movie, a book or a walk in nature may jiggle something inside you that provides the next steps. Trust that the answer will come. But please don't believe that negative voice that tells you that you are worthless and your work is meaningless. Remember that voice is not all of you; it is just a portion of your personality. Observe this part of you with compassion, but don't let it run the show.

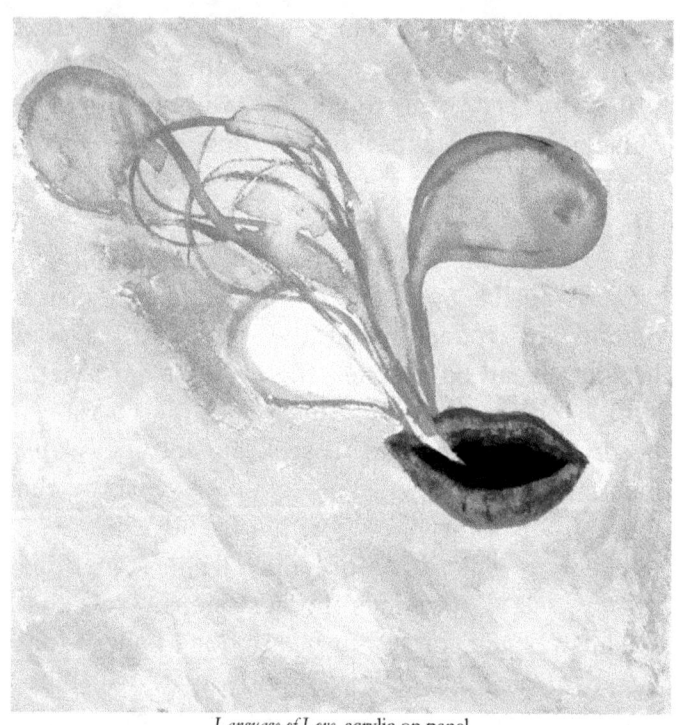

Language of Love, acrylic on panel

4. Cultivate Support and Encouragement

If you study art movements throughout the centuries, artists have always been congregating in guilds and ateliers, cafés and salons, to debate, discuss, exchange ideas and spur one another forward.

Although as an artist most of your studio practice may require working alone, you can't necessarily thrive as an artist in complete isolation. It is unreasonable to think so, and yet so many of us expect exactly that of ourselves. I have learned how essential it is to have support. I value it so highly that I seek out mentors who are further along on their paths than I am for that kind of accelerated propulsion forward that we rarely achieve in isolation. I benefit not only from their wisdom and experience, but the best ones also help keep me accountable to my growth and commitments. Getting an outside perspective on your gifts, achievements, goals and ideas is priceless. By seeking out mentors, teachers and colleagues, and working with coaches and accountability partners, I have become increasingly focused and productive. Having a support network of people who are genuinely interested in your success and achievement and are holding you accountable is invaluable. Sometimes you can find this kind of community in artist co-ops, artist retreats, arts organizations and schools. I built into the Mindful Artist Mentorship Program a community forum because I know the power of this kind of connection.

One Portland, Oregon artist who went through the program, told me, "The community component...is an extremely effective means of gaining a diverse and candid support/critique group. Inspiration and excitement flourish on the group forum." Through following the program curriculum, working one-on-one with me, and with the accountability of the group, she was able to establish a regular studio practice where there had been none and finally complete works that had been in progress for years.

A coach or mentor is another valuable support. Top athletes, singers, actors and dancers all work with coaches and trainers. A president has the cabinet; CEOs have their boards of directors. I have noticed that highest achievers in our society were working with experienced and skilled teams of advisors and coaches rather than trying to figure it all out on their own.

I didn't understand the whole "coaching" niche until recently. I heard about it and took it for some fad or media buzzword, but really didn't know what it was about. Then I had an opportunity to work with a coach I respected and admired. Once I started working with her, I was amazed at what huge shifts I was able to make with her support. Changes that would have happened slowly, if at all, I was able to make quickly with her guidance and insight. I not only had her backing me and holding me accountable but more importantly *believing* in my potential – in some cases more than I was believing in myself. She was able to see potential, opportunities and ideas that I hadn't even noticed. She encouraged me to step into a bigger version of myself. Once she opened the door for me, I would hesitate at first but then step through and become this new version of me, wondering why I had been so afraid before.

Receiving outside support and accountability and wise counsel are the cornerstones of my success strategy. I don't even think of trying to do what I do on my own. Why would I, when support abounds?

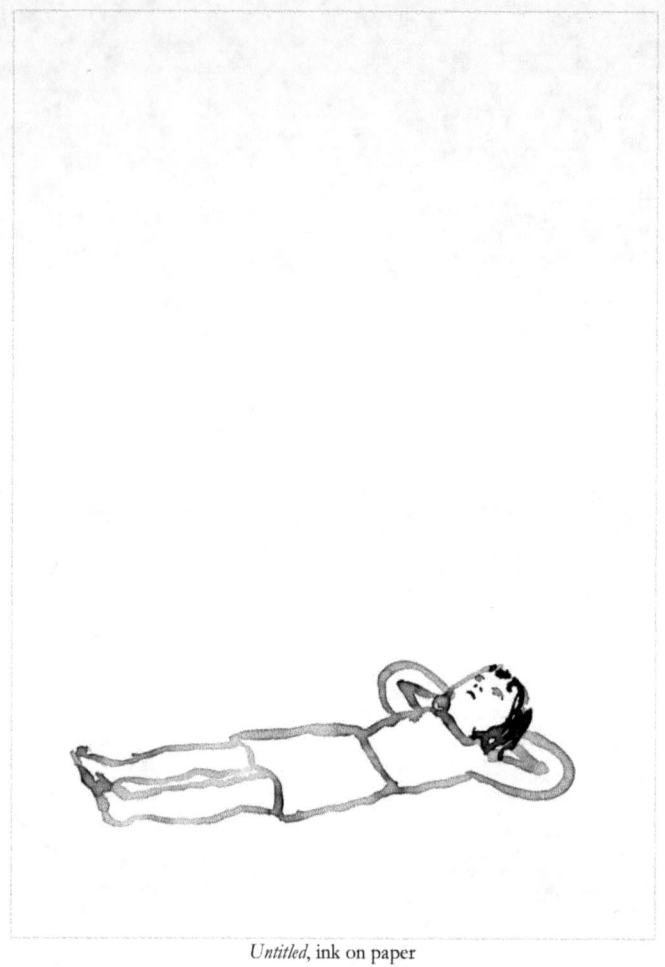

Untitled, ink on paper

5. Maintain the Engine

Your physical and mental health must always come first if you are to maintain a balanced and productive life as an artist. Without your health and well-being you do not have the physical stamina or mental clarity to do the work you love.

Artists are notorious for ignoring their health. I have encountered many artists who routinely take risks with their materials, neglecting to use proper ventilation or protective gear. A startlingly high percentage of artists have suffered permanent disabilities, nerve or immune system damage or even died from using toxic materials and practices.

But it's not just the improper handling and use of toxic materials that can damage artists' health. It can be subtler forms of ignoring the body, not making time to eat well, exercise regularly or get adequate rest.

Artists can also be prone to overworking. Most have some kind of full - or part-time employment outside of their art practice. To make sure they get studio time, they may put in long hours before or after their day jobs. They love what they do so much it can be intoxicating and hard to stop working. Trying to fit too much into our schedules creates undue stress. Stress is the leading cause of health problems in the U.S.

Each artist must negotiate a workable balance between studio time, work, family, play, and rest. Just because you have full-time employment or are occupied with raising a family doesn't mean you can't make a significant body of work. There are countless examples of artists and writers who created whole bodies of work while raising children or working full-time. Many a full-length book as been written in thirty to sixty-minute daily increments.

It is important to remember that your physical body is the engine that drives the machine.

If you don't value taking excellent care of yourself, in the long run, the work may suffer. You may become exhausted, lose focus and mental clarity and become less productive. I've seen artists who are unable to maintain a consistent studio practice rely upon upcoming shows and deadlines to push themselves to work long, exhausting hours only to burn out and collapse afterwards. Perhaps the adrenaline rush of having a deadline and rushing to complete it are exhilarating but the long-term effects of such cycles can be damaging to the body.

Scheduling in non-negotiable time for exercise, eating healthy meals, and seeking quiet, reflective time all help to create a happier, healthier, saner artist who can joyfully meet the physical and mental challenges in the work.

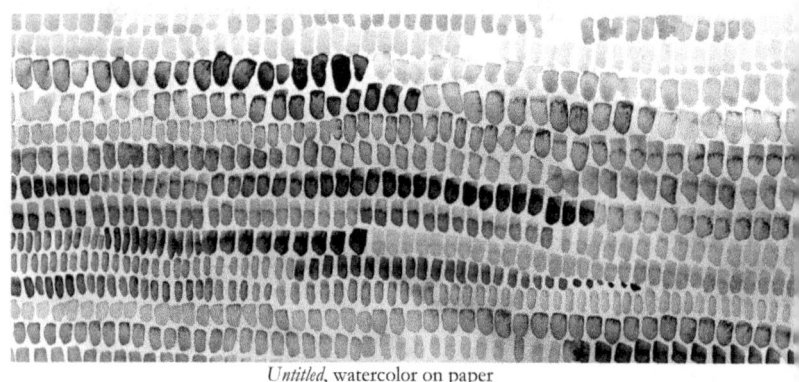
Untitled, watercolor on paper

6. Order and Serenity

Organizing our time, our priorities, our studios and workspaces, our desks, even the files on our computers can be overwhelming and confusing. We miss deadlines, misplace important tools, and get frustrated about having to wade through mess and confusion to even get started.

As an artist you are probably right-brain dominant, so the left-brain traits of linear and analytical thinking necessary for organization may not be your strong suit. Be gentle with yourself and appreciate the creative genius that springs from your right brain. If you have a vibrant, if sometimes messy and disorganized home or studio that is causing you frustration, seek outside help. Your ability to organize your papers, work files, materials, goals and priorities will have a direct impact on your success.

The artists in the Mindful Mentorship Program express a remarkable increase in energy and clarity after our module on organization and de-cluttering. Spurred on by the energy of the group, artists who have had significant difficulties in the past with disorder and clutter make huge strides, freeing up momentous space and time for creative work. By clearing out old, unused and outdated materials, equipment supplies and work, and creating clear, organized workspaces, you will waste less time in the studio. Organizing your computer files, paperwork and images of your artwork, enables you to respond quickly to calls-for-entry and important opportunities and to prepare for a systematic approach to sending your work out on a consistent basis.

A well-ordered workspace facilitates the working process on many levels. I love the kind of serenity that order brings to me. When I walk into my studio and things are put away and easy to access and find, my creative mind feels free, ready and eager to create. The longer I work as an artist the more important it is to have a highly organized structure for my creative output. I have created systems for sorting, organizing, documenting and inventorying my many drawings, installations, sculptures and paintings.

This kind of getting on top of stuff also extends to the big picture, which is so essential to our success. Now, I reflect each year on what I have done so far and look over what I want to accomplish in the studio and in my career in the coming year. I have created a system of checking in with these goals and visions.

I love sharing my systems with the artists in the mentorship program, providing them with templates, worksheets, resources for inventory, goals, mailing lists, etc. It has been amazing to me what a difference it has made for the artists I have worked with to begin to de-clutter and create workable systems in the studio and office.

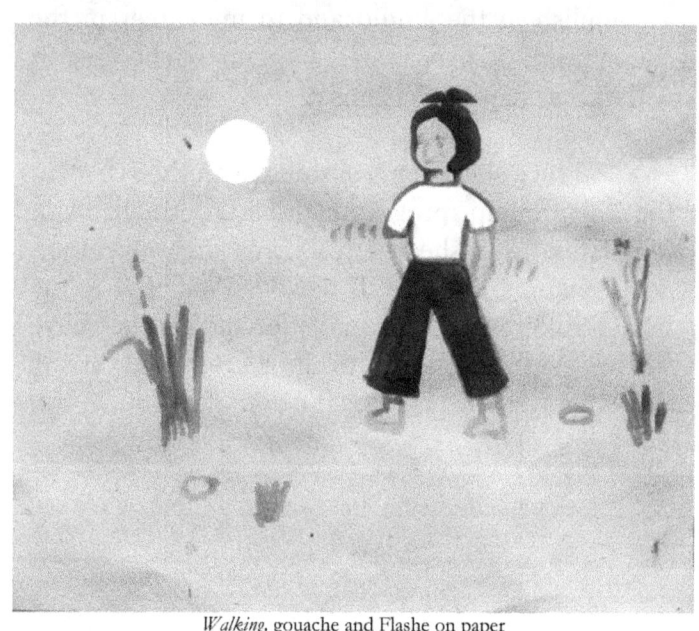
Walking, gouache and Flashe on paper

7. Accelerate Your Progress Through Clear Intentions

The whole concept of intention has had an extraordinary impact on my life. When I have taken the time to set down intentions and create a clear vision for my work and my life as an artist, it is surprising how many of these things have unfolded for me over time with seemingly little effort on my part. I'll even look back years later and see where a written vision statement I had completely forgotten had taken a surprising and even more delightful form than my original intention.

When I first started to work with intention, I didn't even believe in my work enough to *set* goals. Or, I thought that setting goals was something other people did but it felt too restrictive and linear for me. It didn't sound like fun, I was afraid I wouldn't achieve them, wasn't sure they would benefit me. Then, as I started to warm up to the idea, I would set goals, file them away and forget about them, only to find them later and feel regretful that I had missed some deadline. Or, I'd remember an application deadline too late and rush to complete it, stressing myself out in the process and resenting the very competition I wanted to win! Clearly, I needed a better system.

Through trial and error, I found some procedures and tactics that work better with my right-brain visual style than many of the traditional, left-brain methods I had learned about. I am now so much more on top of the goals and deadlines that are important to me. To prevent energy zapping guilt, I've learned to pace myself, prioritizing the important goals and letting go of the ones I don't have time for, without fear or regret.

A fun and effective way to start is by creating big, gorgeous vision for your life.

Where would you like to be with your art in one year? Three years? Five years?

Allow yourself to playfully expand with this vision, unfettered by practicality or your own doubting mind. Remember when you were a kid and you allowed yourself to imagine doing whatever you wanted when you grew up? Most artists don't allow themselves to dream large. We stop ourselves because our ideas seem impractical or unachievable or even embarrassing to admit.

What I teach in the artists in the mentorship program is the difference between the *essence* of an idea and the eventual *form* it will take. The pure essence of any idea can manifest in numerous ways. It's important to learn to discern between the two. Forms are fluid and negotiable, the essence is the core that will remain the same. The essence is the part of the idea that will feed you. For instance, you may have been wanting very much to get into a particular juried show or gallery? But what is it that you *really* want? Greater exposure? More access to collectors? Sales? Affirmation of the value of your work? Recognition from your peers? Now think how many different ways these essences behind the form might come to you.

When you create your life vision as an artist, allow yourself to dream freely and really stretch yourself here, don't worry about exactly *how* you will achieve your vision. It's important to listen to these whisperings, yearnings or longings to know where to point your ship. Give yourself some quiet, uninterrupted time. Write everything you can imagine down in vivid detail. You may also want to express this vision visually. Use color or collage, draw pictures, patterns or symbols to bring your vision to life. Be sure to put the date on this so you can refer to it later.

Next you'll want to engage your practical side. What might it take to bring this vision into reality? There is something of the numinous in how things may unfold, but many of your dreams will require some concrete action on your part. Make a reasonable list of things you would like to accomplish in the coming year. Hold these visions lightly, not tightly. Remember they may happen in a different way than you expected them to. For example, if you would like your work to be seen by more people, be open to where and when that might happen. Could it be on your website or blog in addition to a brick and mortar show? If your overarching vision is to increase your income from your art, be open to what forms that might take: Several small sales? One large sale? Leasing or renting your work? Commissions? Mass production of one image or piece?

Break big visions into small action steps. What is one small thing that can be done today to make this vision a reality? Do you need to do some Internet research? Or pick up the phone and call someone? Write that down on your to-do list and commit to getting it done by a certain date. You don't need to think of the whole project at once.

Too often, we get paralyzed into inaction because our vision is so big, we feel overwhelmed. Just as every piece of art is an accumulation of actions and creative moments, the realization of your goals is simply small, manageable action steps taken one at a time.

Set aside regular and consistent time in your calendar to attend to your vision and goals. Find an accountability partner and check in with each other at least once or twice a month, preferably weekly. Make commitments to each other as to which tasks and goals you will complete before your next meeting. You can meet in person or on the phone. Agree that your time together will be focused on business matters and that you will set aside another time for socializing. At each meeting, follow up with your partner and share upcoming competitions, residencies and grant applications. If you have trouble making decisions about which opportunities to follow up on or which images of your work to send in, ask your accountability partner for advice. It is remarkable how much clarity I gain just from talking an issue over with someone. A decision that had been stymieing me for weeks is often resolved in a matter of minutes.

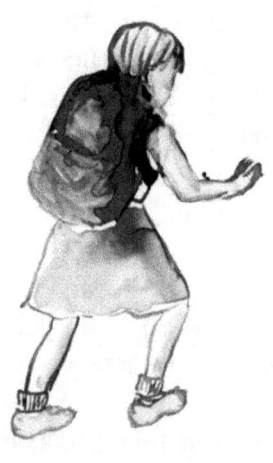

Backpacker, watercolor on paper

Moving Forward

The truth is that this work of being an artist goes very deep. What I am sharing with you in this book are ways of thinking, being, and acting in the world that I have developed through trial and error and refined over many years. It has meant the difference in my life between struggle and anxiety to a sense of joy, satisfaction, confidence and purpose that I wake up with each and every day. Give yourself time and space to make changes at your own pace. There is no urgency and no need for haste. All is well.